The Mountain Trail
and Its Message

Gilmore Lake, near Lake Tahoe, in 1910

The Mountain Trail and Its Message

Albert W. Palmer

with

Introduction and Commentary
by Charles Palmer Fisk

and

Epilogue
by Holly Van Houten

Sixth Street Press
Fresno, California

Photo credits:
pp. 2, 6, 12, 16, 18, 20, 30, 38—Albert W. Palmer
pp. 45, 48, 53, 56, 64, 69, 76, 82, 88, cover—Charles P.
Fisk

Library of Congress Catalog Card Number: 97-066260

ISBN 0-9641404-7-0

This book is printed on 100 percent post-consumer
recycled acid-free paper with soy-based inks. Text is
Adobe Caslon with Goudy Text Lombardic Capitals.
Printed by Jostens, Visalia, California.

Cover by Sharon Scott Design.
Cover photo: Tahoe-Yosemite Trail, between Kennedy
Meadows and Tuolumne Meadows

Pine cone ornaments used with permission of the University
of California Press, from *A California Flora*, Philip A. Munz
with David D. Keck, copyright 1959, The Regents of the
University of California.

Published by Sixth Street Press
3943 North Sixth Street
Fresno, California 93726

Contents

Hetch Hetchy Valley, about 1910
Now partially flooded as a reservoir; O'Shaughnessy Dam
spans the canyon at about mid-picture.

Introduction and Acknowledgments to the Second Edition

When my maternal grandfather, Albert W. Palmer, wrote *The Mountain Trail and Its Message* in 1911, he had only recently begun his long and illustrious career as a pastor, author, and administrator. Throughout a span of more than fifty years until his death in 1954, he brought to every aspect of his work that rare combination of wide-ranging vision and intense practicality that he recorded in this slim volume, the first of his twelve books.

From the multitude of parables that might be derived from reflections on a mountain trail, he carefully selected only five to relate his inspirations to the demands of the daily lives of his readers. He left it to us to ponder the additional parables that his thoughts would awaken in us, each with our unique experiences and perceptions and pathway—or trail—through life. On my life journey, I have referred extensively to his original five parables and added a couple of my own.

Palmer's "simple lessons of the trail" were drawn from his experiences on several Sierra Club outings shortly after the turn of the twentieth century. It is remarkable that they remain just as fresh and valid today, as we stand on the threshold of the twenty-first century, as when they were written eighty-five years ago. Although the setting for his parables was the high Sierra Nevada range in

California, readers can identify them with any wilderness or natural area they have experienced—either personally or vicariously through words, pictures, or imagination.

While the parables are timeless, some of the anecdotes and descriptions Palmer uses in them offer authentic glimpses of early Sierra Club attitudes and practices. Like John Muir, founder of the Sierra Club, my grandfather kept voluminous journals and diaries and took many photographs. In his diary entry for July 1, 1908, he notes that he was fortunate to share a campsite near Muir. A portion of his diary and some of his photographs, as well as a remarkable letter from Muir, are included here. The diary excerpts are taken from his biography, *Albert W. Palmer—A Life Extended*, edited by his daughter, Margaret Palmer Taylor, published in 1968.

My grandfather Palmer gained his insights, reflected on them, reached his conclusions, and acted on them in a wide variety of circumstances and locations. He traveled extensively throughout the world. He lived and worked in Oakland and in Southern California, in Illinois, and in Honolulu. He treasured many summers spent at Indian Cove in Ontario, Canada. The places where he lived and visited, the things he saw, and the people he met provided him an abundant supply of material for his sermons, books, and radio broadcasts, all of

Albert W. Palmer, about 1922

which reached a broad audience and created a rich legacy.

Deep as were his love and respect for the out-of-doors, they were matched or exceeded by his love and concern for all people. Palmer was keenly affected by the turbulence of his times, and he sought ways to improve conditions that troubled him. Observation wasn't enough for my grandfather. He formed strong opinions, expressed them forcefully, and took vigorous action throughout his life. Rather than sitting by and bemoaning the ills of society, he directed his tremendous energy to seeking solutions.

As a liberal minister serving a number of urban parishes, and later as president of Chicago Theological Seminary, he was in a favorable position to become acquainted with a broad range of people— from the humblest worker to an array of national and international leaders. Letters from John Burroughs, Toyohiko Kagawa, and Franklin D. Roosevelt, as well as the letter from John Muir reproduced on page 19, have been preserved in family files.

Unfortunately, much of Palmer's spoken and written legacy is now difficult to access, as tape-recordings and videotapes were not common during much of his life and most of his books are now out of print. So it is a real pleasure to present a new edition of *The Mountain Trail and Its Message*.

   This volume is the result of the combined efforts of three generations of Albert W. Palmer's
descendants. My mother, Margaret Palmer Doane,
her sister, Helen Palmer Sonderby, and her brother,
Philip Wentworth Palmer, all contributed edito-
rial and financial support for this project. As one
of his grandsons, I have deeply enjoyed renewing
my memories of my grandfather as I edited this
edition and wrote a commentary on its text.
Palmer's great-granddaughter, Holly Van Houten,
has added her thoughtful insights in the epilogue.
We invite you to share this documentary and
inspirational work.

Charles Palmer Fisk
Spokane, Washington
Spring 1997

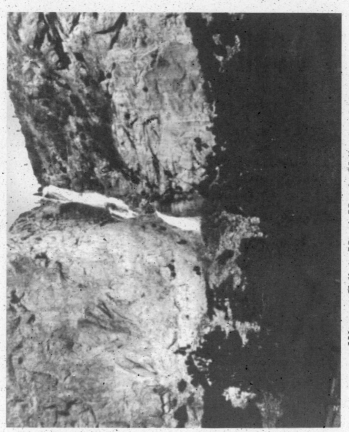

Wapama Falls in Hetch Hetchy Valley in 1910
Today's reservoir, when full, extends about halfway up
the talus slope below the lower falls.

Prologue

An Early Sierra Club Annual Outing
Excerpts from Albert W. Palmer's 1908 Diary

As a graduate of the University of California (1901) and pastor of Plymouth Congregational Church in Oakland (1907–1917), Albert Palmer became well acquainted with Yosemite and the trails of the Sierra Nevada range.

In the Mountains with the Sierra Club

During the summer before Margaret was born, I went on a Sierra Club camping trip and kept a diary. I shall share portions that give a glimpse into the early hiking and camping trips.

JULY 1, 1908
Fish Creek near Little Kern River

We reached Porterville at 4 A.M., had a cup of coffee and then took the stage for Springville. There were 34 rigs for our party. We made the 17 miles to Springville where we had breakfast. At 9 A.M. we started for the Middle Fork of Tule River. Then we started up a steep, hot, dusty trail through the chaparral without a bit of shade or water for three of the longest miles in California. It was hot, hot, hot and steep. We made the three miles in two hours, and at a beautiful place beside the creek, stopped an hour for lunch.

Arriving at camp, found hot tea ready with milk and sugar in cans on convenient rocks. Everybody helps himself and then hunts up his dunnage bag and selects a place to sleep. Soon the sound of a tin pan beaten by a big spoon echoes through the forest and you make for the fire.

You fall in line and come to a stack of tin cups, a graniteware pie plate and a kettle full of knives and forks. You pass on to a group of young women behind boxes on which are kettles of food. The first girl fills your tin cup with soup, the next gives you ham, the next potato, the next corn and the last one stewed dried apricot. Then you help yourself at the cracker box and hunt a soft spot to lean against a log and eat!

After lining up to wash your plate and cup you wander around camp getting acquainted. Then comes a call: "Line up for lunches for tomorrow. No lunches given out in the morning." First you select a paper bag. Then the first man deals you out two hardtack, the next man gives you a hunk of cheese and eight dates, the next gives a can of sardines to every other man. Out of this develops an institution known as "my sardine partner" whom you endeavor to keep in sight the next day.

John Muir is with us and tonight has spread his blankets just below mine under this great old yellow pine. All in all it is a jolly crowd—everybody seems to take things cheerfully.

JULY 8, 1908
Today we left camp at 5:45 A.M. and lunched, after an eight-mile hike, on top of a mountain ridge
8,000 feet high—a rise of 4,000 feet! Got into
camp at 5 o'clock and went down the little creek
one-fourth mile to a little swimming hole.

For lunch tomorrow I have crackers, cheese,
black figs and a hunk of chocolate. Tomorrow we
have a 12-mile tramp mostly through Trout Meadows and on to Little Kern Lake at the beginning
of Kern Canyon where we have permanent camp
for a week.

JULY 9, 1908
We arrived here at 3 P.M. after a fine 12-mile walk.
Forded the Little Kern River in my boots—no
leaks! On a big tree near the kitchen a mail box
has been put up and mail will go out tomorrow
morning. A list of the members of the expedition
has been posted also.

JULY 21, 1908
Kern River Canyon
Miss Harriet Monroe of Chicago read an excellent poem of her own composition on "The Trail"
at the evening campfire.

We held our Sunday Service at the Campfire.
It was a beautiful spot—clean, fragrant pine
needles, the great cliffs and blue sky above. A
Scotch Presbyterian led the singing and I preached

Little Kern Lake
Albert Palmer's Sierra Club group had a
base camp here for a week during July 1908,
when this photograph was taken.

the sermon. There was a large attendance—at least 100!

Last night was "Ladies Night" at the Campfire and we had a lot of stunts. The "Dunnage Bag Ballet" was simply great.

JULY 23, 1908
Mineral King
This morning we rose at 5 and by 6 were on the trail. We climbed to the summit of Coyote Pass; then down to the foot of Farewell Gap. It was a beautiful climb to the summit of Farewell Gap— far away the purple mountains with the blue haze filling the valleys. Near at hand the great peaks of jagged red rock, while the trail ran through a continuous flower garden—solid acres of blue lupines, then scarlet paintbrushes, white Mariposa lilies, blue larkspur, immense cyclamens and many flowers I couldn't name.

Later Entries
CAMPING AT YOSEMITE
The whole family went to Yosemite Valley in the summer of 1910. We reached Camp Curry by a dusty train ride and then by a dusty stage into the valley. Mr. Curry was a big man with a tremendous voice. If folks did not come to breakfast promptly, he would stand outside the dining room and shout: "At eight o'clock the cooks get hot and burn the breakfast toast!" His voice could be heard

throughout the valley and even at Glacier Point high above the camp! I carried Margaret, not quite two years old, "pic-pac" on my back on most of the walks in the valleys.

Margaret Palmer at Camp Curry
in Yosemite, 1910

THE MOUNTAIN TRAIL AND ITS MESSAGE

Each summer I spent a month in the High Sierras as an enthusiastic member of the Sierra Club. I prized the friendship with John Muir and his wisdom about nature. Out of these summer experiences came my first small book, *The Mountain Trail and Its Message*, which was published in 1911 by The Pilgrim Press.

Letter from John Muir

Martinez, Nov. 9, 1908

Dear Mr Palmer:

I Thank You heartily for the Photographs You kindly sent me. The intense mountain light has darkened them rather heavily, but as ~~mementos~~ of our grand outing & its lessons many of them from your sermons, I prize them highly & am

Yours sincerely

John Muir

Martinez, Nov. 9, 1908

Dear Mr. Palmer:
I thank you heartily for the photographs you kindly sent me. The intense mountain light has darkened them rather heavily, but as mementoes of our grand outing and its lessons, many of them from your sermons, I prize them highly & am   Yours sincerely, John Muir

Hetch Hetchy Valley, 1910
View to the northeast from a point
near the present dam.

The Mountain Trail
and Its Message

Albert W. Palmer

I t has been my privilege during the month of my summer vacation for the last three years to be led in paths—paths which have been to me paths of righteousness, of joy, and of inspiration. Out here in the West we call these paths mountain trails. It is out of my experience with these "paths of righteousness" that I seek to bring you the message of the mountain trail.

The trail is not the grandest thing in the mountains—it is only a humble path. It is not the most beautiful—it is often ugly and scarred, filled with dust and stones. But it is one of the absolutely necessary things,[1] and one comes into a peculiar intimacy with it.

There is a vast difference between a trail and a road. There are usually many roads, and if one loses the road he may make inquiries and find another one. But if one loses the trail he must find that one trail again, and there is no one of whom to ask directions.[2]

A road advertises itself afar off. You can always tell when you are coming to a road, but you may pass within twenty feet of a mountain trail and never dream of its presence, so modest is it and so slight. A road looks very much alike mile after mile, but every rod of a mountain trail has an individuality all its own.

One usually travels a road in a vehicle, but I have always traveled the mountain trail on foot, and, traveling so, every rise, every down grade, every stretch of dusty sunshine, every cool shadow becomes important and noteworthy. And so, as day by day you surrender yourself to the mountain trail and follow gladly where it leads, there comes a feeling of peculiar intimacy and companionship with it.

My experiences on the mountain trail have been, for the most part, in connection with the annual outings of the Sierra Club. Our outing parties number from one hundred twenty to two hundred people,[3] and we spend a month each summer in some remote and beautiful part of the Sierra Nevada. All supplies are carried by our hired pack train of mules and horses over mountain trails, for we go into that region where the roads "run out and stop." At night we sleep in the open air in sleeping bags on piles of fir boughs or pine needles or even, after a hard day's tramp, gratefully upon the hard clean ground.

Each person is limited to forty pounds of baggage, which must include sleeping bag, extra clothing, and all personal belongings. This forty pounds must be packed in a dunnage bag three feet long and eighteen inches in diameter, with the owner's name blazoned on the side in letters two inches high.

The cooking is done by Charlie Tuck, a Chinese man. In the winter, Charlie cooks for a hotel in San Rafael, but in his hotel contract he always specifies that he is to have July free to go with the Sierra Club. Charlie has two Japanese men and his nephew, Toy, as helpers, and he rules "the commissary," as the camp kitchen is called, as supremely as ever the Empress Dowager ruled Peking. It is stern and simple fare he gives us—soup and rice and canned corn and tomatoes, fresh meat occasionally, trout in abundance, hardtack, bacon, dried prunes and figs, and, on high days and holidays, a white pasty pudding, with infrequent raisins scattered through it, which the irreverent have nicknamed "Wall-paperer's Delight."

Our party is made up of lawyers, doctors, college professors, high school teachers, and occasionally a rancher, business man, or minister. There are even more temperaments and points of view than occupations. The mountains seem to mean something different to each one.

There is my nephew, the Fisherman—he values each camp in terms of the number of trout that rise to his fly in the adjacent mountain torrent. The Geologist loafs along the trail, oblivious to the very existence of trout, breaking rocks with his hammer; and, after everyone else is in camp, the Botanist drifts wearily in, like an overdue tramp steamer through the Golden Gate, with his press full of flowers.[4] No ancient lava or rainbow trout for his herbarium, if you please!

This man in the well-tailored khaki suit has been planning reservoir sites all day, and that other man in shabby corduroys and a broad gray hat has been watching the shadows in the canyons, listening to the music in the trees, and entering into fellowship with the chipmunks that cheerily share his lunch.

When the day's tramp of from six to eighteen miles is over, we all gather after supper in a great circle around the campfire. Each mem-

ber of the party contributes according to his
ability. There are silent souls that do their share
by keeping the fire a-blazing, there is a Los
Angeles lawyer with an improvised limerick
for every occasion and a Berkeley doctor with
an inexhaustible supply of stories.

The Botanist and the Geologist share their
knowledge with the rest of us, leaving out the
big words, and a quartet, four men from four
corners of the country, sing some of the good
old songs. Last of all "the Signor," with his
head thrown back and his fine spiritual face
illumined by the blazing fire, touches his
violin and pours out in music the things we
all long to say and cannot.

Sunday comes and we gather, men and women of many creeds or no creed at all, under the shelter of some majestic yellow pine with the great cliffs towering above us. The old hymns, led by the violin, the simple prayer, the Twenty-third Psalm repeated together, the sermon touched with a sense of the Divine presence all around us—these things all help to make a summer in the Sierra more than a physical refreshment alone.

And so day by day we live in fellowship with the trees, ever calm, dignified, serene, and with the great cliffs in whose presence we feel so slight and so transitory.[5] And then at night, when the campfire has died away and a hush has settled down across the hills, we lie in our sleeping bags and, before we close our eyes, look straight up at the innumerable and silent stars, and learn anew what it may mean to pray.

Last year a member of our Sierra Club wrote a very beautiful little poem entitled "The Mountain Trail." It has not yet been published and I am not at liberty to reproduce it in print. It tells of how the trail winds its way up the mountainside, through the flower-strewn mountain meadows, across the rushing rivers, up the great rock slopes, and even over the gleaming snow, and closes with the longing that it may go on forever:

Over the misty mountains,
Past the wide heights of blue,
Even to the crystal fountains,
Where all the dreams come true.

I do not wonder that the mountain trail should arouse a poet to song, for I have spent days on the mountain trail which were in themselves like poems lived, and the memory of which is like the echo of some great music. I have started out in the morning and climbed a rocky, dusty trail up steep zig-zags through the chaparral until, hot and weary, I have come to a gently sloping plateau land, where the trail wound slowly upward through fragrant pines with great bronzed trunks and then dipped into little meadows green with springtime and glad with flowers. In the trees birds were singing, and as I listened I said over to myself those

Rodgers Lake, near the Tahoe-Yosemite Trail, north and west of Benson Pass

beautiful lines of Edwin Markham's on "Joy in the Morning":

I hear you, little bird,
Shouting a-swing above the broken wall.
Shout louder yet; no song can tell it all.
Sing to my soul in the deep, still wood;
'Tis wonderful beyond the wildest word;
I'd tell it, too, if I could.

And then I have climbed up above the tree line and, sitting beside a bed of white heather with its exquisite white and crimson bells, have looked across the jagged peaks and gleaming snow drifts of the summit region. Below, a blue little lake with solemn trees around it; yonder, a lake still frozen over, with a snow bank reaching down to it like a miniature glacier; and everywhere the beautiful French-gray granite cliffs, so clean that they make one feel as if all sin and stain had been swept from this upper world forever.

And then I have crossed the pass and gone down the other side, reached camp, and again felt the joy of companionship and home.

A Parable of the Higher Life

I find in the mountain trail many parables, but first of all a parable of the higher life. The mountain trail life involves hardship. The trail is far beyond the reach of wagon roads. No luxurious cars carry one around its curves. No one leans back on the cushions of an automobile along the mountain trail. He who would know the trail must leave the comforts and luxuries of civilization behind, must be glad to wear great heavy hobnailed shoes, strong simple clothing, must be ready to live laborious days, to lie down at night weary on the hard ground, to eat plain food and to share in the hard work of camp life.[6]

If a man will do this the trail shall bring him great rewards—a clear atmosphere such as the valley people never know, the beauty and majesty of mountain fastnesses which the people in the luxurious trains see not, and, when the roads where the automobiles speed along are lined with dust and sunburned grass, the trail will lead him into little nooks where the flowers are yet in springtime.

Is this not a parable of life?

There are men who live their lives on the wagon roads, in the Pullman car, on the cushions of an automobile. They shun all hardship; their object in life is to avoid all pain, just to have a good time. And they have their reward—miles of dusty road, acres of sunburned grass.

But there are other men who live the life of the mountain trail, the life of aspiration and endeavor. They are

Pioneer souls who blaze their paths
Where the highways never ran.

They hear something calling them out of the unseen even as Kipling's Explorer heard

One everlasting Whisper day and night
repeated—so:
"Something hidden. Go and find it. Go and
look behind the Ranges—
Something lost behind the Ranges. Lost
and waiting for you. Go!"

They, therefore, consecrate themselves not to the common dusty roads of material comfort and pleasure, but to the quest of the ideal.

It means oftentimes a loss of comfort, it means poverty perchance, it may mean defeat, as the world counts defeat, to follow this trail of the ideal. But it is the men who have lived such lives who have moved the world, and they have not been without their reward—beautiful flowers bloom for them which the men on the dusty road below know not of.

I have found myself this summer often thinking of Jesus' saying, "I am the way." What a splendid trail of the ideal his life has blazed across the mountains of this life! What joy of the mountaineer comes to those who follow in that trail!

A Parable of Our
Indebtedness to the Past

No man can walk mile after mile
over a mountain trail without a feeling of gratitude toward the men who made it.
Resting beside the trail one day I found myself thinking of the Indians who first found
the pass; of the rough pioneer soldiers under
Kit Carson or some other fearless leader who
may have been the first white men over the
route; of the cattlemen who made it easier and
plainer; of John Muir in his rugged youth, traveling alone with his flour and his tea, and without blankets that he might carry more food
and thus be able to penetrate farther into the
fastnesses of the Sierra and bring back to the
people word of the wonders and beauties he
had seen. I thought also of the foresters who
had rebuilt the trail and of the troopers who
guarded it.

Into a sense of grateful fellowship with all
these men one enters as he lives day by day in
companionship with the mountain trail—this
long slender thread which, stretching back over
the hills, seems to be the only thing connect-
ing him with civilization and, leading on into

the unknown, promises new joy and beauty
for the days to come.

And with this gratitude goes a duty—the
duty not in any way to injure the trail, but, as
far as possible, so to place a stone here or re-
move one there as to improve the trail and
make it plainer and easier. In high altitudes
the trail goes over the bare granite, where there
is no way of marking its location except by
low piles of stones, called "ducks," placed at
frequent intervals. It is an unwritten law of
the mountains never to destroy a "duck," but,
rather, to add another stone.[7]

What a parable it is of our heritage of human institutions and ideas! These customs and
institutions are the trails across the mountains
of time built by those who went before us. The
family, the state, the Church, law, religion,
standards of honor and conduct—they are all
great trails to find and mark on which our
ancestors ever since before the dawn of history have labored.

How wise are those who treat these things
in the spirit in which the mountaineer treats
the trail! The true mountaineer does not start
off cross country regardless of trails.[8] He
knows difficulties and dangers will confront
him if he does. It may seem strange that the

trail goes down here or up there, but he stays
by it because he knows that the men who built
the trail must have had reasons for their course.
And so he follows the trail and sees that it is
in no way injured or obscured.[9]

More than that, he improves the trail. He
realizes that no trail is perfect. He puts a log
across a bad stream crossing, and if a tree has
fallen across the trail he chops a way through
it or around it. He may even, with better sur-
veying instruments and with dynamite to blast
the rocks, find and build a shorter and better
grade. But through it all the old trail is the
basis on which he works, and he never forgets
or despises the men who made it.

Happy the man who follows this parable
in regard to human ideas and institutions; who
seeks not to destroy but to fulfill; who, when
he seeks to reform the social order, realizes the
heroic service that was given to bring to pass
even the imperfect freedom and justice we have
today; who, when he criticizes the Church,
appreciates also the work it has done and is
doing for the world; who, when he reaches a
sweeter and simpler creed, remembers that the
creeds of the past, however rough and crude
and harsh, were yet trails over which men traveled on to fellowship with God.

Head of Tuolumne Canyon, 1910

A Parable of Companionship and Personal Worth

Again there comes to me a message from the companionship of the trail. No man passes any other upon the trail without speaking to him. Strangers will stop and exchange information about good camping places. The standards of value and judgment are different from those on the great roads below. Men[10] are not valued according to their wealth at home. No one cares who your father was or what club you belong to. Neither is judgment based on outward appearances. The man with the shiniest shoes or newest fangled kind of knapsack is not the man most honored on the trail.

The trail has different standards. It honors and respects and yields obedience to character and the capacity and willingness to do. The man who does his share of the work without grumbling, the man who does the cooking, the man who contributes his talents to the common good modestly and cheerfully, whether his particular talent be catching trout, telling a good story, running the pack train, frying hot cakes, or playing a violin in the light of the campfire so that the cliffs echo back such music as they never heard before—whatever the talent may be, there is the man who is honored and respected on the trail.

And if but one humble and obscure man on a mountain trail be lost, every other man on the trail feels in duty bound to aid in the search till the lost is found. One night two of our party failed to come into camp. As searchers started out on horseback how gladly we contributed little articles which might be of service! How anxiously we waited until an hour later two shots far down the canyon told us that both the lost ones had been found![11]

What a magnificent thing if we could bring this companionship and these standards down into the city street!

How fine to keep up that feeling of brotherhood which, in the spirit of Walt Whitman, silently at least, salutes every man we meet! How fine to keep on judging people, not by their clothes or their wealth or social standing, but by character! How fine if we could awaken in the great roaring city, with its saloons, its brothels, its gambling dens, that mountain responsibility for seeking and finding those who go astray!

A Parable of Sauntering

There is a fourth lesson of the trail. It is one which John Muir taught me. There are always some people in the mountains who are known as "hikers." They rush over the trail at high speed and take great delight in being the first to reach camp and in covering the greatest number of miles in the least possible time. They measure the trail in terms of speed and distance.

One day as I was resting in the shade Mr. Muir overtook me on the trail and began to chat in that friendly way in which he delights to talk with everyone he meets. I said to him: "Mr. Muir, someone told me you did not approve of the word 'hike.' Is that so?" His blue eyes flashed, and with his Scotch accent he replied: "I don't like either the word or the thing. People ought to saunter in the mountains—not 'hike!'

"Do you know the origin of that word 'saunter?' It's a beautiful word. Away back in the Middle Ages people used to go on pilgrimages to the Holy Land, and when people in the villages through which they passed asked where they were going, they would reply, 'A la sainte terre,' 'To the Holy Land.' And so they became known as sainte-terre-ers or saunterers. Now these mountains are our Holy Land, and we ought to saunter through them reverently, not 'hike' through them."[12]

John Muir lived up to his doctrine. He was usually the last man to reach camp. He never hurried. He stopped to get acquainted with individual trees along the way. He would hail people passing by and make them get down on hands and knees if necessary to see the beauty of some little bed of almost microscopic flowers. Usually he appeared at camp with some new flowers in his hat and a little piece of fir bough in his buttonhole.

Now, whether the derivation of saunter Muir gave me is scientific or fanciful, is there not in it another parable? There are people who "hike" through life. They measure life in terms of money and amusement; they rush along the trail of life feverishly seeking to make a dollar or gratify an appetite. How much better to "saunter" along this trail of life, to measure it in terms of beauty and love and friendship! How much finer to take time to know and understand the men and women along the way, to stop a while and let the beauty of the sunset possess the soul, to listen to what the trees are saying and the songs of the birds, and to gather the fragrant little flowers that bloom all along the trail of life for those who have eyes to see!

You can't do these things if you rush through life in a big red automobile at high speed; you can't know these things if you "hike" along the trail in a speed competition. These are the peculiar rewards of the man who has learned the secret of the saunterer!

A Final Parable

There is one last parable which the mountain trail brings to me—its endlessness. It climbs to the crest of the ridge and is lost to sight, but it goes down the other side. It loses itself in the green depths of the canyons below, but far away on the other wall, if your eyes are clear and strong, you can make it out zig-zagging up out of the canyon again.

You camp for the night weary beside the trail, but the trail runs on as a prophecy that you too shall follow in the morning.

Only once have I followed a mountain trail to its end, and that was when we climbed Mount Whitney.[13] There, fourteen thousand five hundred feet above sea level, at the very highest point in the United States,[14] the trail seemed to end at a rude pile of stones. But do you know, I believe the poet saw the deeper truth, and I too believe that there is a trail that still leads on

    Over the misty mountains,
    Past the wide heights of blue,
    Even to the crystal fountains,
    Where all the dreams come true.

Scouts encounter switchbacks on Seavey Pass,
on the Tahoe-Yosemite Trail.

Commentary and Notes

Editing *The Mountain Trail and Its Message* involved only a few minor alterations and required very little time. But many of the expressions that my grandfather used, as well as themes he mentioned but did not develop in his brief work, have proven very stimulating to my thoughts. So I have directed my efforts toward a commentary in the form of footnotes to those ideas and expressions that intrigue me most.

Each reader will perceive a mountain trail, or, for that matter, a trail in whatever setting, through his or her own particular lens. The lens through which I look some eighty-five years after the parables were written focuses on several issues that hardly existed, or seemed of minor importance, in 1911. Palmer touches on such problems and issues throughout his five parables, but he focused his particular lens on the relationship between the physical and the spiritual pathway.

A parable is usually simple, direct, and quite specific in the truth or moral lesson it seeks to impart. Because a parable is so brief and focused, it challenges the listener or reader to explore the wider—perhaps even contradictory—ramifications of the premises it accepts, as well as the possible consequences of its application. Just as I have been stimulated by my grandfather's parables, I hope my comments will stir readers to focus and act upon the most pressing problems they encounter as they engage in their quest for the "higher life," the subject of his first parable.

In the narrative preceding his parables and in his diary, Palmer mentions several of his companions on a Sierra Club outing. In the second parable, he pays stirring tribute to his predecessors on the trail. Whether such people were explorers of physical realms, such as John Muir, or illuminators of the spiritual realm, such as Jesus the Christ, Palmer emphasizes the debt of gratitude we owe to those who have laid the trails we follow.

My grandfather ranks high on the list of those I admire most: those who have not only heard the call to service but who have also responded to it vigorously. Among those who have spoken most eloquently and acted most effectively for the wilderness in my lifetime are Aldo Leopold, Bob Marshall, Sigurd Olson, David Brower, Edward Abbey, and David Foreman. Some have been controversial, others more serene. In matters of the spirit, Teilhard de Chardin, Thomas Berry, Matthew Fox, and Michael Dowd have emphasized the mystical and spiritual aspects of ecology and stewardship of the earth. I recommend that readers of this book delve into the writings of both groups of challenging thinkers.

Scouts on the John Muir Trail
in the vicinity of Mather Pass

Scouts on the Tahoe-Yosemite Trail in the vicinity of
Kennedy Meadows, where the trail follows
an old prospectors road

Notes

1 (page 22). My grandfather's choice of the expression "absolutely necessary things" with regard to hiking a mountain trail leads me on a variety of paths as I consider the implications of the terms "absolutely" and "necessary." I found myself questioning what he meant by the use of those two words, and what problems their use raises.

In his straightforward declaration about the absolute necessity of a trail, Palmer leaves it to the reader to consider all the other necessities for traveling a trail—and the parables for living that may be derived therefrom. For example, most hikers today use a guidebook, often in conjunction with a map and compass, for help in finding their way. Likewise, every faith has its sacred texts and traditions that help the seeker to chart a course to the "higher life" of the soul.

On a truly difficult trail or climb, or on an expedition, a guide and/or a number of support personnel, such as Sherpas in the Himalayas, may be employed. Similarly, every faith has its saintly souls to point the way when the going gets rough, and organizational support is available in congregations of like-minded seekers of the way, to whom one may turn instead of following a solitary path. Palmer speaks eloquently to this "companionship of the trail" in his third parable.

As I consider aspects of the absolute necessity of a trail in the mountains, whether in the physical or spiritual sense, I find myself confronting three major issues: desirability, accessibility, and convertibility. Throughout the footnotes, I will refer to various points of view about them.

The very presence of a manmade trail in a wilderness or natural area, no matter what its size, alters the character of that area to some degree. Such a presence poses the problem of the desirability of locating a trail there in the first place.

Wild animals and ancient tribes used the majority of routes over land and sea and through the mountains of the North American continent long before the arrival of audacious and ambitious white men. In many instances the new settlers did little or nothing to alter or "improve" the existing footpaths.

In his parables, Palmer accepts a condition of semi-development of a mountain trail that is adequate or even comfortable for many who spend time in the mountains. But, as wilderness and natural areas continue to shrink in size and people press ever farther into once almost inaccessible mountain areas, many wilderness enthusiasts are troubled by any efforts to build new trails or even to maintain those that already exist. Some advocate reverting to "cross-country" travel, getting away from overcrowded footpaths whenever possible or practical.

In his second parable my grandfather refers to some of the potentially positive and negative consequences of leaving a trail. On the one hand, I've been fortunate to feel on rare occasions the indescribable mixture of joy and exultation, tinged with sadness, that is almost overwhelming, mystical in its impact. I've felt it when looking into a high alpine basin or a colorful nook in a canyon that I've reached without a path to follow. With soaring spirits and sparkling eyes, I've thought, "Wow! I wonder how many people have seen this before!"

Joy and exultation result from my success, yet there is sadness in knowing that the moment can't last—and that not many hikers will be able to experience what I've been so lucky to see or do. I've felt such a moment in the red glow of sunset, while sitting on a lofty ledge overlooking a vast darkened valley, watching jagged streaks of lightning rend banks of thunderheads. I've felt it while lying in my sleeping bag at the foot of the trail to Rainbow Bridge. In the shadow of that vast arch cast by the silvery moonlight, I knew that the place where I lay would soon be flooded by the rising waters of Lake Powell.

On the other hand, I've felt on rare occasions (fortunately) that paralyzing mixture of anger and frustration, tinged with hope, that can be equally overwhelming. I've felt it when I've blundered onto a cliff I could neither ascend nor descend and was forced to retrace my steps, or when I've thrashed through a thicket of chaparral (that dense, almost impenetrable brush that cloaks the middle heights of the Sierra Nevada). With ripped clothing and scratched skin, I've thought, "Whew! I wish I hadn't taken this route!"

Anger and frustration result from my carelessness, yet I feel hope because I know this circumstance can't last—and perhaps others won't follow the same misleading route. Having wandered without sufficient bearings among high peaks and maze-like canyons, I know the profound relief of returning to an established trail. So it is in life. Each person must fashion his or her own best compromise between striking out away from the beaten path or sticking with it wherever it leads.

One compelling reason for not tramping cross-country is the potential for damaging fragile ecosystems. The crushing and bruising of plants and shrubs caused by even a single passage, not to mention the injury inflicted by scores of feet, hooves, or tires, can wreak havoc. Whether to the tiny plants of an alpine meadow or the cryptogamic soil of the seemingly barren desert, heedless transit can leave scars that take years to heal. In a similar manner, sensitive human spirits can be damaged by the consequences of callous speech or action, whether intentional or not. How often I've realized that I should "get back on track!"

A potentially deleterious effect of a trail is that it tends to "funnel" or confine travelers to a narrow corridor. In some sensitive areas, deep trenches or ruts may form, leading to erosion and siltation problems. Hikers in some places have made a series of parallel paths or "braided" trails to avoid the accumulation of dust or water in the original pathway, but the results of such a practice pose their own set of very real problems.

Palmer acknowledges that some trails are poorly located and must be abandoned or relocated.

On the Tahoe-Yosemite Trail in the vicinity
of Matterhorn Peak

Parallel ruts in the Tahoe-Yosemite Trail
in the vicinity of Bond Pass

Constant reassessment is required to determine the timing and means of such closures or relocations.

There is a possible parable here for our daily lives as well. Occasionally we may find ourselves mired in the ruts of our habits or fettered by our outmoded customs and traditions. At times we may be confused by a plethora of choices. At such times we may have to proceed carefully and prayerfully if we are to discern and choose the best possible trail.

In view of his unbounded admiration of those who traveled without trails, with only hints or visions of what might be, to guide them, I find it puzzling that Palmer used such a strong declaration as "absolutely necessary." Certainly neither he nor John Muir envisioned the sheer numbers of people who now answer Muir's clarion call to "climb the mountains and get their good tidings." Indeed, Muir's and the Sierra Club's mission for many of the early years was to publicize and promote the "use" of wilderness by traveling into it in large groups.

The impact of such large parties—250 or more people camping in one spot on Annual Outings such as those that formed the framework for my grandfather's trips—aroused some controversy even then. So the question persists, and will only become sharper, as to whether a trail is desirable if it attracts hordes of people to pass through an area best left undisturbed.

The problem of accessibility involves many difficult decisions as we draw closer to the twenty-

first century. Accessibility to whom, and how
many? For how long, and in what areas? In what
seasons, and for what purposes? By which means,
and in what manner? These are by no means all
the vexing questions that must be answered.

In his parables, my grandfather presupposes a
relatively hardy, healthy, mature person with a sense
of curiosity about the out-of-doors and a desire to
satisfy it by means of an experience removed from
the general conditions and amenities of civilization—but not too far away! Hence the use of pack
animals to transport vast quantities of food and
gear during his Sierra Club Annual Outings.
Palmer expresses his own preference for foot travel,
but there are those who swear that real pleasure is
possible only on horseback or with the support of
pack animals.

In Palmer's time, problems of access for people
with physical and other kinds of disabilities were
not recognized or tackled to the extent they are
now, however imperfectly. A perception that wilderness areas are accessible only to the "able" or
"financially elite" causes considerable strife between
those who would restrict access and those who
would encourage it.

I am sure John Muir would shudder at what
has happened to some of the trails located along
lakeshores or across high, open meadows—his
beloved "sky parlors." He was well aware of the
damage that sheep and pack stock could cause
in fragile areas, having been a sheepherder for a
time himself. In addition to the sheep, cattle,

On the High Sierra Trail approach to Eagle Scout Peak

mules, and horses of his day, today's hiker may encounter mountain bikes, off-road and all-terrain
vehicles, snowmobiles, and exotic animals such as
llamas. (Llamas are used as pack animals in some
areas because their impact on the environment is
not as great as that of traditional stock.) Like the
question of trail development, the question of
whether access to wilderness and natural areas
should be increased or curtailed continues to be
vigorously debated.

A third major issue my grandfather's parables
raise is that of the potential for the conversion of a
mountain trail into something far different from
its original condition. Once a trail has been dis-
covered or created, a steady progression may follow—from simple trail to the rough wagon road
of Palmer's day, and from there to the deeper trail
of today's rugged four-wheel drive vehicle, the
paved road, and eventually the superhighway. A
railroad grade may parallel or replace the trail, and
a flight path may overarch it.

The history of all continents is replete with
examples of this kind of progression; whether it
represents progress is open to debate. The Oregon
and California Overland Emigrant trails, the Santa
Fe Trail, El Camino Real linking the Spanish mis-
sions in California, the routes of the Lewis and
Clark expedition, of the French Canadian
voyageurs, of David Thompson and Alexander
McKenzie across Canada—these are just some
examples in North America.

The existence of a trail presupposes some destination, goal, or greater opportunity *to* which it leads. The concept of mountains as a destination for their own sake has emerged relatively recently in human history. Indeed, most trails were built in an effort to get *through*, or better yet, *around*, mountains. Many early travelers regarded trails as trials and terrors, as some of them truly were. Others felt great enjoyment on them. Most experienced a combination of trial and enjoyment, as people do today, that my grandfather knew and expressed so well.

One of the early conflicts in the Sierra Nevada range was whether or not to build the Tioga Road in Yosemite National Park, replacing ancient Indian trails with a gravel (and later paved) road on which one could travel at a speed of fifteen miles an hour! Arguments continue over the nature and location of trans-Sierra roads. So the vexing question persists, and will become sharper, as to whether a succession of improvements is inevitable as people seek to travel faster and more easily.

Perhaps the greatest potential for harm to wilderness areas and their trail networks comes from human development. The devastation of the Hetch Hetchy valley, north of and roughly parallel to the Yosemite valley, for use as a reservoir, was only a precursor of the wholesale onslaught by hydroelectric power developers to come. Two historic photographs (on pages 6 and 12) taken by my grandfather show the beauty that existed in the Hetch Hetchy valley before its flooding.

The widespread destruction of vast tracts of forest land—including groves of Muir's beloved sequoia or redwood trees—by clearcutting continues at a frightening rate. Open pit and strip mining despoils the land, resulting in surface- and groundwater pollution. Twice I have been halted in my tracks by ominous signs warning, "Private land. No trespassing. Danger: Cyanide in Use Ahead." These nightmares of the future posed no threat to the serenity my grandfather felt on the mountain trails of his day, although great "monitors" or water nozzles had already been used to tear out huge swaths of land to get at California's gold.

Nor would Palmer have experienced, as I once did on the summit of Mount Whitney, the howl of U.S. Navy jets "at play" about a hundred feet overhead. Their sonic booms nearly knocked some climbers from their perches on Whitney's sheer walls, and they frightened many who had not seen or heard their supersonic approach. Most of us were enraged by this invasion of our quiet by such noise pollution. I will admit to being amused, once the shock had worn off a bit, by the spectacle of the planes diving and barrel-rolling *below* me, as they swooped over the deep Owens Valley to the east.

After a number of us lodged complaints, the Navy promised not to carry out flights directly over the summit in the future. Until very recently the issue was still controversial in the Grand Canyon of Arizona, where aerial maneuvers by military jets and the frequent clatter of commercial helicopters shattered the peace and silence of its depths. New regulations have been adopted concerning minimum altitudes for flights over the canyon.

Yet another threat to existing trail systems is the encroachment of human habitation. The old route of the emigrants' wagons, including those of the Donner Party on a segment of the Truckee River route of the California Emigrant Trail, now pass through a golf course, lawns, and gardens; houses have been built on *top* of the trail in places. Donner Summit exhibits a prime example of trail conversion. It has not only foot paths and jeep trails, but also an eight-lane interstate highway, a railroad and power lines transmission corridor, several ski lifts, and a flight path overhead! Little serenity there!

On the Appalachian Trail near Hanover, New Hampshire, my boyhood home until 1951, the Velvet Rocks shelter used to be at least a half-hour's hard hike from town. In 1996 it took me only about ten minutes to reach it from the nearest street.

Urban sprawl threatens to engulf enclaves of natural areas and the trails that run through them. The Sierra Club and many other organizations have entered into countless frays over access to and development of our land. The matter comes down in part to a question of whether we want mountains like the European Alps, laced by the cables of tramways and ski lifts and covered with tourist resorts, or something in a more natural state. The conflict is constant and ongoing.

Lest my grandfather's five cogent parables become lost in the welter of problems I have raised, I feel that each reader needs to accept the trails he or she knows in any area—large or small, rural or urban, wherever they are found. Trails need to be cherished, protected, and walked—or sauntered—with the joyful attitude that my grandfather proposes in his fourth parable, that of appreciation, not speed.

2 (page 22). Not until 1934, when *Starr's Guide to the John Muir Trail and the High Sierra* was published, was there an adequate description of the Sierra Nevada trails, and even that covered only a portion of the range. Since then a host of fine books has become available dealing with mountain trails and experiences on them.

The United States government has undertaken stewardship and promotion of the National Trails System. Three great long-distance trails—the Appalachian Trail in the East, the Pacific Crest Trail in the West, and the Continental Divide Trail along the spine of the nation—continue to be augmented by others, forming a great network of paths that future generations may follow. The reader is urged to use a library or visit a mountain shop to learn more from the guides and descriptions available.

Some trails have been completed, while others are still in developmental stages. Relatively recently there has arisen renewed interest in the many waterways and canoe trails that were once used so prominently in the exploration of our continent. For many people the strokes of a canoe or kayak paddle in calm or white water are as satisfying as strides along a mountain trail—with or without a backpack! While it might seem that threats to waterways are not as severe as those to land pathways, nevertheless they do exist. May all participants in their outdoor experiences develop parables that speak to their particular needs, and may they be shared with those who follow, as my grandfather suggests in his parable of companionship.

3 (page 24). The potentially destructive impact of large parties on wilderness areas was recognized in the late 1970s. The number of individuals or size of groups entering at many trailheads and in other areas is now strictly regulated.

4 (page 26). Picking flowers and gathering speci-
mens is now forbidden in national parks and
monuments, but not in national forests unless pro-
hibited by provisions of the Endangered Species
Act. When my grandfather took the outing described here, the U.S. Forest Service had been in
existence for only six years. Gifford Pinchot, its
first administrator, had formulated his policies of
"multiple use," defined as "the greatest good for
the greatest number in the long-term," and "on a
National Forest the present and future *local* de-
mand is always considered first."

Although modified since Pinchot's time, these
are still the prevailing policies governing use of
the national forests. Because of the general nature
and inclusiveness of the policies, they are the subject of continuing controversy—some instances of
which have reached the Supreme Court. To this
day national forests are administered by the Department of Agriculture, whereas national parks
and monuments are administered by the Department of the Interior.

The concept of public parks is not new in the
United States. Almost every New England town
and eastern village had its "common." Central Park
in New York City was created in 1857. Frederick
Law Olmstead, landscape architect of the park,
thought it "would humanize the city and soften
its hard edges through nature." The federal government had set aside a small area at Hot
Springs, Arkansas, as early as 1832. This was
followed by the granting of federal lands in the

Tahoe-Yosemite Trail
in the vicinity of Seavey Pass

Yosemite valley and the Mariposa Grove of Big Trees to the State of California in 1864 to administer as a state park, as protection from the already potent threat of commercial logging.

The Yellowstone region in Wyoming became the first park to be designated as "national" in 1872, following the strenuous efforts of an exploratory group known as the Washburn-Langford-Doane expedition. It was not until 1906 that the State of California re-ceded control of the Yosemite area to the United States, making it the second national park.

Both Yellowstone and Yosemite had suffered under highly uneven management and poorly defined purposes, at times under the supervision of the U.S. Army! Both faced almost insuperable assaults from cattle and sheep herders, mining and timber exploiters, and poachers, among others. Because of their locations, both were perceived as prime sites for reservoir construction. In the case of Yosemite's Hetch Hetchy valley, the park lost. The conversion of Yosemite from state to national park status happened in part because of a three-day visit to the area by President Theodore Roosevelt in 1903, hosted by John Muir.

It was not until 1916, some five years after publication of Palmer's book, that the National Park Service was created. Its first director, Stephen T. Mather, was charged by Secretary of the Interior Franklin Lane to: "maintain (the parks) in absolutely unimpaired form . . . to be set apart for the use, observation, health, and pleasure of the people

. . . and the *national* interest must dictate all decisions affecting public or private interest in the parks."

The first two policies are, of course, frequently at odds with one another, while the third stands in sharp contrast to the policies of the U.S. Forest Service. It is somewhat ironic that one of the most climactic battles waged by the Sierra Club, over the issue of a dam proposed for location in Dinosaur National Monument in Utah, was caused in part by conflicting interests and jurisdictions between the Bureau of Reclamation and the National Park Service, both agencies of the Department of the Interior. The Sierra Club's drive to defeat the Echo Park Dam won the day in that instance, partially offsetting the loss of Hetch Hetchy.

But a far greater calamity was to befall wilderness with the construction of the Glen Canyon Dam and the creation of Lake Powell on the Colorado River in Arizona and Utah in 1963. There are those who maintain that Lake Powell is no calamity at all, that its waters open a vast area to pleasure boaters that formerly was accessible to only a very few hikers or boaters.

The stories of both the U.S. Forest Service and the National Park Service are well told in a number of books. Another somewhat lesser known entity, the Bureau of Land Management, part of the Department of the Interior, is responsible for vast tracts of federal lands not included in military or Indian reservations or administered by either the U.S. Forest Service or the National Park

Service. The trails that lead to and through lands managed by the Bureau of Land Management are as fraught with controversy as are those administered by the other two agencies.

5 (page 28). I find it somewhat curious that my grandfather does not mention the awesome fury of High Sierra thunderstorms. I have encountered them frequently in my mountain sojourns. John Muir gloried in nature's occasional fierceness. He recounts a stirring incident in which he climbed a tree to experience more fully the elemental forces unleashed by a furious windstorm on one of the ridges high above a tributary of the Yuba River north of Yosemite. He perched in the tree for several hours "like a bobolink on a reed," while the tree "flapped and swished in the passionate torrent, bending and swirling backward and forward, round and round, tracing indescribable combinations of vertical and horizontal curves." Why he was not killed during this or others of his hair-raising exploits one will never know. Like Benjamin Franklin with his kite and key, Muir was probably courting death. But both survived with increased knowledge of and respect for the power of natural forces.

Judging by his lyric description of calm days and tranquil nights, it may be that my grandfather did not want to frighten away those whom he sought to entice to sample the glories of the High Sierra for themselves. Or perhaps he personally encountered only the long periods of benign weather that can grace the "range of light." But no one who ventures into the mountains should go unprepared for the possibility of severe weather. I have had more than a foot of snow fall on my tent during one night in mid-August! I learned later that three members of a group at a neighboring lake, who were less prepared than my Boy Scout group, had died of exposure during that storm.

6 (page 32). Travel on trails is considerably more comfortable eighty-five years later, at least with regard to clothing and gear. With the advent of high-tech fibers, foods, and equipment, a person can manage with much less weight than that endured by earlier hikers.

Most visitors to the mountains do not try to subsist on a diet such as Muir's, that often consisted of tea, flour, raisins, and oatmeal for days at a time. The hobnailed boots of early hikers have

A scout on the High Sierra Trail approach to
Kahweah Gap and Eagle Scout Peak

Scouts from Troop 266, Tahoe City, California,
on Benson Pass, Tahoe-Yosemite Trail.

been replaced by lighter footwear with soles designed to cause less wear and tear on fragile trails. Hobnailed boots, as well as horseshoes, have the effect of scarring, scratching, and grooving the highly polished glacial surfaces of rock traversed by some portions of mountain trails. With a good sleeping pad and groundcloth, there is little need to suffer on hard ground. Our lighter weight fabrics make layering of clothing more efficient now than it was in my grandfather's time.

7 (page 36). The crossing of bare granite is discussed in the preceding note. The practice of placing "ducks" in open land or blazing trees along forested portions of a trail has been the subject of considerable criticism in recent years, particularly when "ducks" are added by uncertain hikers.

I have encountered situations in the Grand Canyon where so many paths have "ducks" marking them that it has become difficult to determine the best route. On the Donner Summit portion of the California Emigrant Trail there are so many blazes and signs placed by people with differing theories of the location of the "original" trail that one must pick and choose which ones, if any, he or she will follow.

On the other hand, the quartz and feldspar capping stones of the cairns (as "ducks" are called in the eastern states) on a portion of the Appalachian Trail near the summit of Mount Washington in New Hampshire were probably all that prevented a miserable night from becoming truly dangerous.

My small group of Boy Scouts was overtaken by darkness and fog while trying to reach the Lakes of the Clouds hut during one of my early forays into the White Mountains. In the pitch darkness, the gleaming whiteness of the cairns, lighted by our feeble flashlights—as well as a lantern thoughtfully left lighted by Hutmaster Brooks Dodge—served to guide us to safety. Many another hiker can tell similar stories about strategically placed blazes or trail markers.

8 (page 36). I find this statement one of the most contradictory in my grandfather's book, especially in light of his admiration for John Muir and his tributes to trailmakers expressed earlier. In striving to make his point about the importance of a trail, Palmer did not clarify his definition of a "true" mountaineer.

There are those who would assert that a "true mountaineer" would have nothing to do with trails, except perhaps as a means of easier access to the real goals of mountain-climbing: the cloud-swept summits or the climbing routes to be found on their walls and faces.

Yet I find it difficult to substitute an adequate adjective for "true." People who go to the mountains run the gamut from those who seek solitude from crowded trails and campgrounds to those who would be very uncomfortable without the feeling of support, safety, and companionship found along well-established paths.

I'm not sure that in his use of "true" Palmer made sufficient provision for those sturdy individualists who do not, or did not, follow existing ways, whether physical, social, intellectual, moral, or spiritual. I referred to this problem, from a somewhat different angle, in my first note. Certainly no future trails will be created without the pioneer who ventures into the unknown or "boldly goes where no man has gone before." Are those who follow on and benefit from the mountain trail any more or less "true mountaineers" than those who first found and marked that trail?

9 (page 37). Probably the most urgent dictum now is not to short-cut on switchbacks on an *established* trail. Such a practice of cutting between the loops of a gently graded trail can result in severe erosion problems.

10 (page 39). I think my grandfather used the term "men" in the broad general sense used in his time for all people, with no disparagement of women, or children, for that matter, intended. Had this book been written today, Palmer would no doubt cite the participation of both women and children in wilderness experiences, as many of both went on even the earliest Sierra Club outings. A charming photograph of my mother, taken in 1910 at Camp Curry in the Yosemite valley, is included on page 18. It shows her as an almost-two-year-old dressed in the best mountaineering tradition.

11 (page 40). Getting lost is one of the most frightening experiences a cross-country hiker can have. Palmer refers to this in his third parable. Over the years, a number of rules have been developed for hikers to follow when they have lost their bearings. The first and foremost rule is not to panic. One should stop and sit down when one first experiences the unsettling feeling of possibly being lost. Children, and even adults, are advised that it may be desirable to hug a tree in order to keep calm and prevent the impulse to strike out blindly in any direction.

I was once caught by darkness while hiking in the Selkirk range of Idaho, and lost the sketchily marked trail. I sat huddled beneath a thick Ponderosa pine until daybreak. Although I didn't actually hug the tree, I was grateful for its protective shelter. The sense of stability it provided me was similar to that image of a tree to which Holly Van Houten refers in her epilogue.

The idea of organized search-and-rescue units and the Ski Patrol system were far in the future when Palmer wrote this book in 1911. Controversies about philosophies to guide and policies to follow with regard to accessibility to natural areas of our nation persist to this day and may well become more acrimonious in the future. How well "qualified" in survival techniques must one be to travel in the mountains? Medicines for use in first aid were rudimentary in my grandfather's day. Although compasses were standard equipment, detailed and accurate topographic maps—not to mention the global position locaters and CB radios available to even the casual hiker, if he or she can afford them—were years away in 1911. Should they now be considered "required" items?

We must reach workable compromises between the two polar opposites of locking up wilderness areas—denying access to everyone, or at most allowing only those with urgent reasons to intrude—and opening them up wide to everyone without restrictions of any kind. While such decisions are admittedly difficult now, they will become even more so if we put off making them as our population continues to increase. If a route to a wilderness or natural area exists, must a trail to it, or through it, be developed? Is it inevitable that a road or rail access must follow? These are tough choices.

12 (page 42). I am not sure if this anecdote appears in Muir's work or in other works about him. It might well be a unique observation of Muir's knowledge of word derivation.

The John Muir Trail descending from
Forester Pass, elevation 13,200 ft.
Only Trail Crest Pass, at 13,600 ft., is higher.

13 (page 44). By 1931 the magnificent trail that bears Muir's name had been built between Mount Whitney and Yosemite Valley, so the summit was no longer the end of a trail. Subsequently the Tahoe-Yosemite Trail was created along a network of park and forest trails, and still later the Pacific Crest Trail provided extensions enabling the hiker to traverse the entire distance from Mexico to Canada—or vice versa. So-called "thru-hikers" prefer to go from south to north because they can start in the relative coolness of spring in the southern deserts and finish before the winter snows arrive on the Canadian border between Washington and British Columbia. Although I have hiked (or sauntered) the four hundred miles plus between Mount Whitney and Lake Tahoe, I and most of my acquaintances have preferred to travel the distances by overlapping loops, utilizing the many lateral approaches as well as the main-stem trail length.

I find my grandfather's assertion that a mountain trail is essentially endless is valid. Not only are most trails connected into networks or webs that offer boundless opportunities for exploration, but a trail's aspect changes from moment to moment and season to season, so that travel is rarely, if ever, repeated. The directions one is traveling— horizontally or vertically, or by compass degrees— change the perspectives of a trail, as Palmer noted.

And so it is true of life, particularly if one believes in an ongoing existence beyond death. Just as a mountain trail may cross a divide or ridge and one cannot see what is on the other side, each of us walks our particular trail in life. Although pain is frequently present, we rejoice in moments of joy and walk our path with hope and faith, in the assurance that it will lead to a splendid destination.

In the words of the old Appalachian folksong, "Lonesome Valley," "nobody else can it walk it for us; we have to walk it by ourselves." Yet each of us must share portions of our life trails with others with whom we are bound in an intricate network on this incredibly beautiful Earth that we call home.

14 (page 44). With the admission of Alaska as a state in 1959, Mount Denali, the "High One" in Native American language, named Mount McKinley by white settlers, topped Mount Whitney. At 20,320 ft. it is the highest point in the nation as well as the highest point in North America.

Epilogue: Trails to the Future
Holly Van Houten

Albert Wentworth Palmer, my great-grandfather, saw his task, as a minister and educator, to frame religion and spirituality in new ways in order to speak to an era he viewed as impatient with tradition. He believed nature provided a way to think about God and religion with a new freedom and from new premises. Nature, he believed, would inspire one to ask oneself what were fundamentally religious questions: "What is the meaning of life? Whence came we? Whither are we going? Is the universe friendly? How shall a man come into right relations with it? What is the meaning of suffering? Is there help in the face of defeat, tragedy and death?"[1]

His book, *The Mountain Trail and Its Message*, was written to recount time he spent in the Sierra Nevada wilderness as well as to describe how such experiences lead to deeper understanding of spirituality and life's purpose.

Wilderness travel, as Palmer describes it, involved considerable hardship, especially before space-age lightweight packs, tents, and sleeping bags. Yet he writes that those who endured such hardship would experience great rewards. He likens the quest for an ideal to attaining a high vista—difficult, yet ultimately vastly rewarding. The trails are just as steep today, physically and spiritually, as when he trod them. And his parables still provide inspiration for working in our own communities to create places of peace and refuge, and to make our relations with others just and right.

His appreciation for and wonder about nature are timeless lessons, as is his encouragement to remain mindful of the beauty around us. The description of meeting John Muir on the trail foreshadows the modern-day bestsellers that tell us to slow down and simplify our lives. Muir and my great-grandfather wanted people to saunter instead of hike. The word "saunter," Muir explained, derived from "sainte terre" or Holy Land, and referred to a way of moving along a trail with reverence. Nature can be a gift of silence, solitude, awe, and contemplation for those who slow down enough to experience it. For Palmer, this slowing down and assuming an appreciative air was a first and important step in seeking out answers to life's great questions—and for finding joy in the ultimate mystery of it all.

Another enduring lesson from the book, but one we hear less about today, is to take the sense of renewal, comfort, and peace gained from retreat in nature and put it to use to improve relations with others and ameliorate conditions within society.

Palmer saw many lessons in the trail beyond the spiritual need for peaceful retreat. In the friendly companionship of the trail he saw a putting aside of differences of class, race, and gender and an honoring of character, hard work, and individual contributions to a greater good instead. He saw an indebtedness *to* and interdependence *with* others, those who came before to build the trail as well as those on whom one must rely for the support of food, shelter, care, and companionship.

Mountain trails were not, for my great-grandfather, simply "paths of joy." They were also "paths of righteousness." They provided a parable for leading a higher life. He saw his role as a minister not only to be sensitive to spiritual values but also to be linked to the practical tasks of life. Following a spiritual path did not stop at finding personal peace and solace; it continued toward seeking personal and society transformation. In biblical traditions, Jesus, Moses, and others did not wander in the wilderness simply in order to return refreshed and relaxed—as if they had just been to some elegant desert spa. They returned transformed by their experience and convinced of a direction to take to improve society.

At home in Oakland, California, where he was minister of Plymouth Congregational Church, Palmer set about engaging his congregation in the social issues of his day. A church historian described him as "the slender young man who revolutionized the nature of Plymouth's activities."

Scouts from Troop 266 clearing trailside brush on the
Angeles Crest Trail near Mount Baden-Powell, named
in honor of the founder of Scouting

One of John Muir's beloved "sky parlors" with
a badly rutted portion of the John Muir Trail
in the vicinity of Benson Pass

One such activity was to establish recreation facilities for young people in the community. "This was the heart and soul of his enterprise," the history continues, "to extend not only a religious fellowship to adults and small children on Sundays but to make his church a social center where, during the week, he might bring the young people and thus combat the influences of poolrooms and saloons."

Another example of Palmer's social activism was the publication of an article in 1919 arguing that the city should purchase a farm and employ inmates from the city jail to work on it, thereby providing prisoners an opportunity to repay their debt to society and learn the value and importance of hard work in the out-of-doors.[3]

The Mountain Trail and Its Message served another purpose in addition to telling a parable of the higher life. Although it is not mentioned in the text, the book was originally published in the middle of John Muir's fight to save Hetch Hetchy Valley from being flooded for a drinking water reservoir for the City of San Francisco. This beautiful valley was arguably as lovely as Yosemite, as Palmer's photographs attest. John Muir's words leave no doubt as to his view of the religious importance of this land: "As well dam for water-tanks the people's cathedrals and churches, for no holier temple has ever been consecrated by the heart of man."[4] Palmer's book could be viewed as putting some religious might behind Muir's muscle and providing inspiration for his urban congregation to join the fight against the damming.

My own personal experiences, quite apart from our family relationship, confirm for me that the lessons set forth in this book have an enduring and timeless quality. Despite a family history that included more than one minister, I was raised outside formal religious institutions and rejected for a time anything that smacked of religion. In my late twenties, struggling with the questions that inevitably come with young adulthood—career, commitments, and life purpose—I was encouraged to find an image, a mental stress-reliever, for use in troubled times. At such moments I thought of a tree—swaying in the wind, yet rooted, and was comforted. I began spending more time in nature, seeking quiet and solitude, and began hearing questions. What was I meant to be doing? What purpose could there be for my presence on Earth? What should I do with my daily life to bring it in concert with that purpose?

Seeking answers to these questions brought me around to making changes in my life—just as my great-grandfather had predicted. These changes included beginning a spiritual practice with the Religious Society of Friends, or Quakers. Another change I made was to resume my work in community planning, this time in a position working to protect open spaces and develop trails, as my

way of giving back to the world around me. You
can imagine the impact of reading *The Mountain
Trail and Its Message*, soon after making these
changes, having heard nothing about the book
prior to my late twenties. Here, just when I needed
it, was something written by a family member
eighty years earlier speaking exactly to what I had
just experienced! I hope reading his words has also
brought recollections of your own experiences.

Later in his life, my great-grandfather wrote
something that could just as appropriately be said
about our own era, more than sixty years later:

> [T]his age of ours peculiarly needs to wor-
> ship. We are so driven by the various pres-
> sures of life that we need a time of refuge
> and peace. We live so much in man-made
> cities where there are no hills to which we
> may lift up our eyes, that we need some
> spiritual sanctuary where our upward-quest-
> ing vision may see a light shining on spiri-
> tual hills and mountains.[5]

From my own work in community planning,
I have found that peace and refuge, as well as transformation, can be just as available in our cities as it
is in the most "pristine" wilderness area. They can
be found in neighborhood parks and nearby nature preserves. They can be found in one's own
backyard. They can also be found where they are
least expected. Through my work, I have come to
know people who are working to protect small

patches of green and others fighting to reclaim abandoned industrial sites as places for residents of nearby communities to enjoy.

In Los Angeles, for example, a park along the Los Angeles River, across from a freeway and railroad yard, in the midst of deteriorating buildings and gang violence, has become a little patch of holy ground for residents of the surrounding community, their own patch of green, closely guarded and well loved. There is no graffiti here, and children play happily in the small grassy areas. The presence of this park teaches the residents, and me, by association, the value of hard work, companionship, interdependence, and appreciation advocated by my great-grandfather eighty-five years ago in his parables of the wilderness mountain trail.

Examples like this can be found in many U.S. cities today as people begin to reclaim vacant or polluted land, or restore creeks as places for fish to swim and children to play. Not only are people seeking a natural place of refuge near their own homes, they are also transforming their own lives and the lives of others to obtain it. They are finding community together, fighting injustice, transforming their neighborhoods, and treading their own spiritually engaged paths.

Just as Albert Palmer and John Muir used their love for the land, and their belief in its ultimate value, to argue for its enjoyment and protection, perhaps you too will be moved to fight for your

own patch of holy ground. We have included a list
of resources to help you learn more about protecting open spaces and developing trails. I hope you
have found this small book as peaceful, resonat-
ing, and ultimately challenging as I have.

Holly Van Houten
San Francisco, California
Spring 1997

1. Albert Wentworth Palmer, *Paths to the Presence of God.* The Pilgrim Press, 1931. This book
contains a series of lectures given while Palmer
was President of Chicago Theological Seminary.

2. Arthur Arlett, *History of Plymouth Church,*
Oakland, California, November 1933.

3. *Should the City Own a Farm?* published in
1919 with preface by Oakland Mayor Frank Mott.

4. Quoted in David Douglas, *Wilderness Sojourn:
Notes in the Desert Silence,* Harper and Row, 1987.
His source was Roderick Nash, *Wilderness and the
American Mind,* New Haven, Yale University Press,
1982.

5. *Paths to the Presence of God.*

On the Hop Valley Trail in
Zion National Park, Utah

Biographical Notes about Contributors to the Second Edition

Albert W. Palmer was a prolific writer who encouraged his three children to follow his example. His first daughter, Helen, is a gifted poet who has published a volume of poetry. She spent nineteen years as a psychiatric social worker, addressing a host of pressing social concerns.

His son, Philip, now retired, was a dedicated pastor who served parishes in both the United States and Canada. His dissertation, "Five Ways to See Jesus," written about 1940, provides insights into the historical and spiritual nature of Jesus.

Palmer's second daughter, Margaret, is a leading innovator in the field of sacred dance. While married to my father, Chester Ballou Fisk, her work was featured in the March 8, 1948 issue of *Life* magazine. The article described her creativity in religious dance, or "the art of rhythmic choirs," as she called it then to allay fears of conservative congregations suspicious of dancing as a form of worship. She wrote five books as Margaret Fisk Taylor while married to architect and professor Walter A. Taylor. Her last husband, Clarmont P. Doane, a distinguished surgeon in Fresno, California, provided security and encouragement as she continued with her writing and leadership of the Sacred Dance Guild. With Dr. Doug Adams of Pacific

School of Religion as editor, she reprinted two early books and wrote two new ones encouraging people of all ages and abilities to use religious dance. She now resides in Spokane, Washington.

As Albert Palmer's grandson, I have inherited his legacy of love of nature and the out-of-doors. His concern for ethical and social conditions helped shape my attitudes and activities. He and his wife, Sara Wedd Palmer, imbued me with a love for plants and animals, especially birds, during the many summers I spent with them at Indian Cove in Ontario, Canada. My grandmother's college major was biology, and she patiently and lovingly taught me to observe and identify the many species that abound there to this day. From my father, Chester, I seem to have inherited much of my wanderlust. He was an ardent traveler and photographer. I gained much of my appreciation for both from him. It was my father also who helped me to decide on a career as a teacher in junior and senior high schools and eventually in a community college.

It was my joy and privilege to live in the heart of the Sierra Nevada range at Lake Tahoe and in the Feather River country of northern California for some twenty-seven years prior to moving to Spokane in 1986.

Like my grandfather before me, I value my membership in the Sierra Club. I have participated in many of its trips and served for many years as a leader on the national committee for river-rafting. Much of my wilderness experience has been gained through membership and leadership in the Boy Scouts of America. I cherish the wealth of friends and memories this organization continues to provide me.

I owe both my parents a debt of gratitude for encouraging me to write. From my earliest efforts in high school, through my college years, to the publication of my first book, they have offered countless good ideas and advice, as well as financial support. My book, a bibliography entitled *Collecting Scouting Literature,* was published in 1985 in collaboration with Doug Bearce and with help from his wife, Robyn. A revised and expanded edition was published in 1990, and a third edition is in preparation.

Holly Van Houten is the great-granddaughter of Albert Palmer. She lives in San Francisco and works for the National Park Service as an outdoor recreation planner in the Rivers, Trails and Conservation Assistance Program, working with communities to protect open spaces and develop recreational trails. She is a member of the San Francisco Friends Meeting, part of the Religious Society of Friends (Quakers). She would like to thank the librarians at the Oakland City Library History Room for assistance, and the Friends in Unity with Nature Committee for inspiration.

References

There is a far wider selection of literature about mountains and their trails than existed in Albert Palmer's day. It will be increasingly easy to access through the Internet and the World Wide Web. Works listed here are some of those I have enjoyed the most and which have proven most useful to me as I've followed my particular trail.

CLASSICS OF THEIR KIND

Abbey, Edward. *Desert Solitaire*. New York: McGraw-Hill, 1968.

Fletcher, Colin. *The Complete Walker*. New York: Alfred Knopf, 1984.

Manning, Harvey, ed. *Mountaineering: The Freedom of the Hills*. Seattle: Mountaineers, 1967.

Olson, Sigurd. *The Singing Wilderness*. New York: Alfred Knopf, 1956.

Reid, Robert Leonard. *Mountains of the Great Blue Dream*. New York: Farrar, Straus & Giroux, 1991.

USEFUL TRAIL GUIDES FOR THE WEST

Starr, Walter A. Jr. *Starr's Guide: Guide to the John Muir Trail and the High Sierra Region*. San Francisco: Sierra Club Books, 1977.

Winnett, Thomas. *Guide to the John Muir Trail*. Berkeley, CA: Wilderness Press, 1984.

Winnett, Thomas. *The Tahoe-Yosemite Trail*. Berkeley, CA: Wilderness Press, 1986.

Winnett, Thomas. *The Pacific Crest Trail, Volume I: California*. Berkeley, CA: Wilderness Press, 1973.

Winnett, Thomas. *The Pacific Crest Trail, Volume II: Oregon and Washington*. Berkeley, CA: Wilderness Press, 1973.

Winnett, Thomas, et al. *Sierra South*. Berkeley, CA: Wilderness Press, 1990.

Winnett, Thomas, et al. *Sierra North*. Berkeley, CA: Wilderness Press, 1991.

BOOKS ABOUT THE SIERRA CLUB

Cohen, Michael P. *The History of the Sierra Club, 1892–1970*. San Francisco: Sierra Club Books, 1988.

Turner, Tom. *Sierra Club: 100 Years of Protecting Nature*. New York: Abrams, 1991.

ABOUT JOHN MUIR

(In addition to his own many books, most of which are still available in reprinted editions)

Badè, William Frederic. *The Life and Letters of John Muir*. Boston: Houghton Mifflin, 1923.

Clarke, James Mitchell. *The Life and Adventures of John Muir*. San Francisco: Sierra Club Books, 1980.

Editors of Country Beautiful. *The American Wilderness in the Words of John Muir*. New York: Country Beautiful, 1973.

Fox, Stephen. *John Muir and His Legacy—The American Conservation Movement*. Boston: Little, Brown and Company, 1981.

Jones, DeWitt, and Tom H. Watkins. *John Muir's America*. New York: Crown Publishers, 1976.

Silverberg, Robert. *John Muir: Prophet among the Glaciers*. New York: G.P. Putnam's Sons, 1972.

Wolfe, Linnie Marsh, ed. *John of the Mountains*. Boston: Houghton Mifflin, 1938.

———. *Son of the Wilderness: The Life of John Muir*. Boston: Alfred Knopf, 1945

ABOUT ENVIRONMENT AND THE SPIRIT

Berry, Thomas. *The Dream of the Earth*. San Francisco: Sierra Club Books, 1988.

Brower, David. *Work in Progress*. Salt Lake City: Gibbs Smith, 1991. A Peregrine Smith book.

Dowd, Michael. *Earthspirit: A Handbook for Nurturing an Ecological Christianity*. Mystic, CT: Twenty-third Publications, 1991.

Fox, Matthew. *Creation Spirituality: Liberating Gifts for the Peoples of the Earth*. San Francisco: Harper San Francisco, 1991.

————. *Original Blessing: A Primer in Creation Spirituality*. Santa Fe, NM: Bear & Co., 1983.

————. *The Coming of the Cosmic Christ*. San Francisco: Harper & Row, 1988.

Gilliam, Ann, ed. *Voices for the Earth*. San Francisco: Sierra Club Books, 1979.

SPECIAL SERIES

I recommend highly any of the volumes in the American Wilderness Series published by Time-Life Books, especially *The High Sierra*, 1979.

The National Geographic Society, through its Special Publications Division, has some excellent volumes related to Palmer's book:

America's Magnificent Mountains, 1980.

John Muir's Wild America, 1976.

Pathways to Discovery: Exploring America's National Trails, 1991.

The Pacific Crest Trail, 1975.

Additional References
Suggested by Holly Van Houten

Nature and Spirituality

Douglas, David. *Wilderness Sojourn: Notes in the Desert Silence.* San Francisco: Harper and Row, 1987.

Emerson, Ralph Waldo. *Nature and Other Writings.* Boston: Shambhala, 1994 (original version of the essay "Nature" published in 1836).

Developing Trails and Protecting Urban Open Spaces

American Hiking Society and the National Park Service. *Tools for the Trail: A Resource Bibliography.* Washington, DC: American Hiking Society and the National Park Service, 1994.

Fink, Charles A., Robert M. Searns for The Conservation Fund, and Loring Schwarz. *Greenways: A Guide to Planning, Design, and Development.* Washington, DC: Island Press, 1993.

Gibson, Penelope. *Community Trail Planning: A Training Handbook.* San Francisco: Bay Area Ridge Trail Council, 1991.

Larabee, Johnathan M. *How Greenways Work, A Handbook on Ecology.* Rivers, Trails, and Conservation Assistance Programs, National Park Service and Quebec-Labrador Foundation's Atlantic Center for the Environment, 1992.

Mantrell, Michael A., Stephen Harper, and Luther Propst. *Creating Successful Communities: A Guidebook to Growth Management Strategies.* Washington, DC: Island Press, 1989.

Moore, Roger L., Vicki LaFarge, and Charles L. Tracy. *Organizing Outdoor Volunteers*, Second Edition. Boston: Appalachian Mountain Club Books, 1992.

National Park Service. *Economic Impacts of Protecting Rivers, Trails and Greenways*. San Francisco: National Park Service, 1995.

Roberts, Mary J. *In Support of Trails: A Guide to Successful Trail Advocacy*. San Francisco: Bay Area Ridge Trail Council, 1993.

Ryan, Karen-Lee, ed. Rails-to-Trails Conservancy. *Trails for the 21st Century: Planning, Design, and Management for Multi-Use Trails*. Washington, DC: Island Press, 1993.

Smith, Daniel S., and Paul Cawood Hellmund. *Ecology of Greenways, Design and Function of Linear Conservation Areas*. Minneapolis: University of Minnesota Press, 1993.